revelations

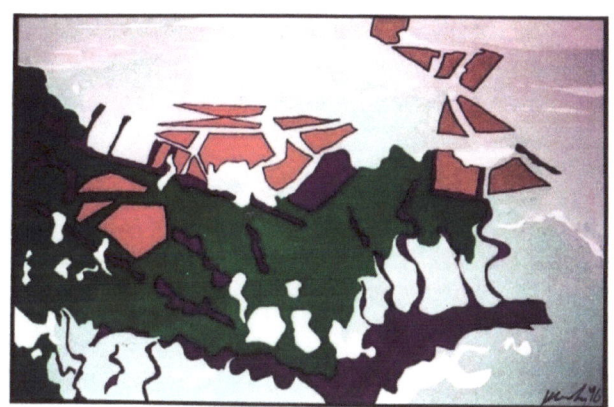

Copyright 2012 by Karen Klosky
Second Edition Copyright © 2017

All rights reserved, including the right to reproduce this book or portions thereof in any form whatsoever.
For information address:

Klosky Creations
1110 15th Ave. West
Bradenton, FL

ISBN-13: 978-1977789235
ISBN-10: 1977789234

Back Cover design by Al Musitano

Manufactured in the United States

Preface

Karen Klosky is an accomplished musician, songwriter, and poet; foremost, however, she is an incredible visual artist. Klosky is tall and elegant, colorful, quirky, creative, eccentric, and bohemian. As a working and dedicated artist, she has traveled and shown her work through a National Endowment for the Arts grant and exhibited in Sarasota's Ringling Museum—an unusual feat, for few local artists have had that invitation. She's that good.

Klosky is a powerful life force, jamming bodhisattva, hostess with the mostess, cat lover, preserver of nature, and she's Christmas all year long. As an artist, Klosky is political, poignant, and urgent. Her mixed media, what this book effects, explores personal themes, such as her own spirituality, philosophical fairness, issues concerning humanity and the natural world, and the current climate of political injustice.

I first met Klosky when I was managing editor of a weekly newspaper on Anna Maria Island, one of the inhabited barrier islands along Florida's West Coast. She wrote a weekly arts column about the local scene for my newspaper. That was a number of years ago, but Klosky continues her involvement in the local arts scene, and she lives in Bradenton's Village of the Arts.

In a state known for its transients, con artists, and scams, Klosky has been a consistent, good, dear friend for years and remains a stalwart Florida flower.

For a while, Klosky and I had a band we called Dr. Klosky and Triage. Guest musicians would sit in at our gigs, and we performed many original songs. Afterwards, we'd go back to her house, partying and playing until the early hours.

I'm in Colorado for a couple of years, but one of the things I look forward to the most when I visit Florida is to see Klosky. She hosts a few jam sessions every year, and anywhere from 60 to 150 people might show up. That's because when it's at Klosky's house, the jam becomes both a dynamic celebration of local music, and life itself.

Despite the fact that it's not as easy to stay up all night as it used to be, when we go to Klosky's, time disappears and playing all night is just something we do.

    Tomara Kafka
    Naropa University, Boulder, Colorado

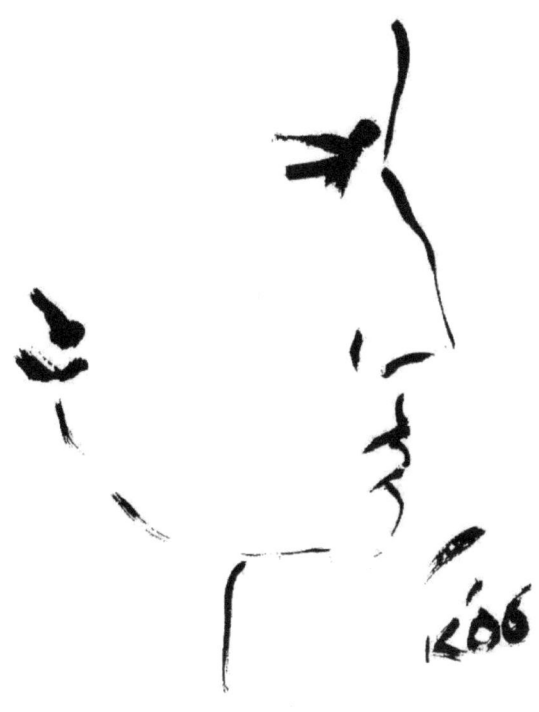

©2006 Karen Klosky

zen

**want
what
you
got**

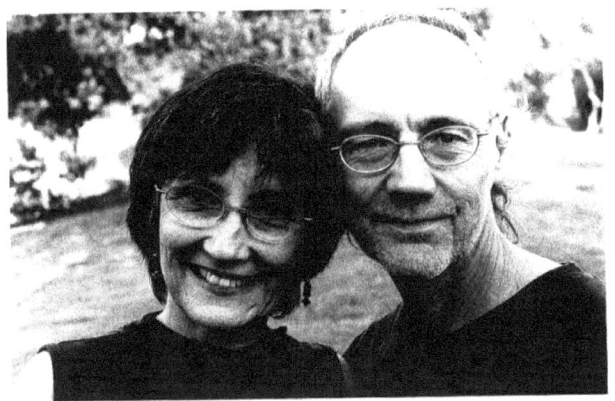

©2000 Karen Klosky

your
eternity
is
right
now

yero

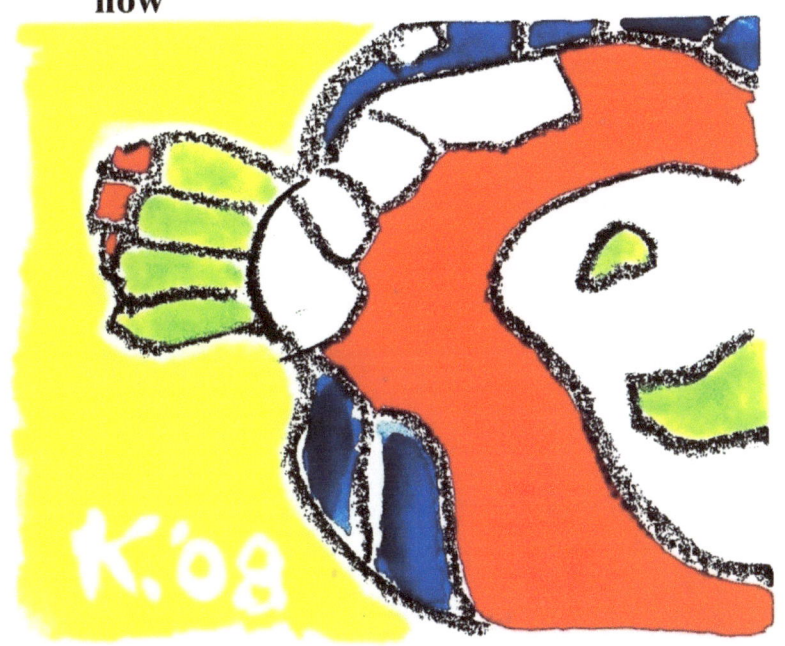

**war
is no way
to live**

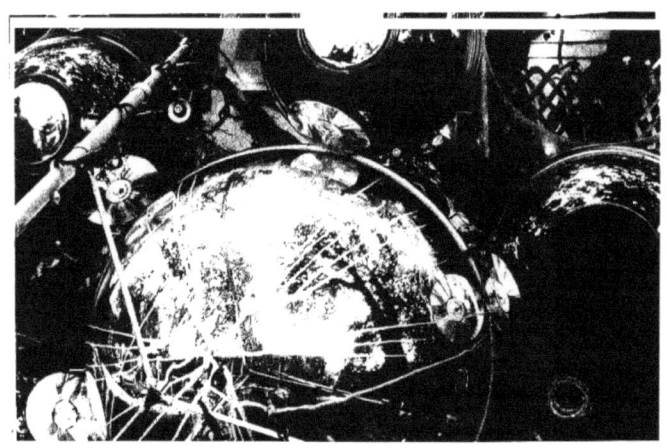

© 2004 Karen Klosky

**child abuse
hurts
everyone**

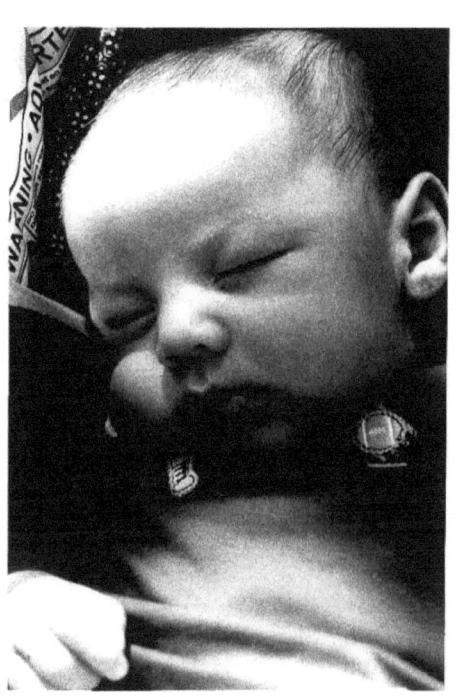

© Karen Klosky 2004

poems

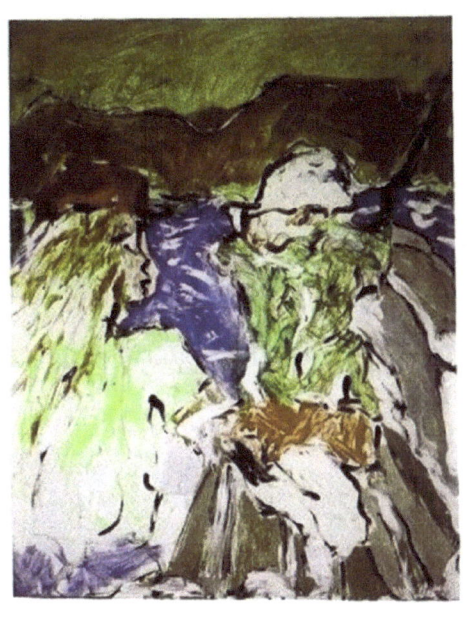

did you know?

i accidentally
sold my soul
to the a m radio
i tossed away
my life one day
for a flame
that burned inside me
i threw my love around
and lost my head
now i have to pay the price
and get it on again
i did it all in vain
and nothing did i gain
thinking life was all a song
a game that continued
on and on

© 1980 Karen Klosky

i remember you then

i went away
that was a mistake
you went away
that was just fate
i needed a friend
it turned out to be him
now the blood has all dried
and i'm still alive
i think of you then
and remember when
our kiss
in eternal time

© 1979 Karen Klosky

the past

---

making finger
drawings
on my steamy
backyard
windows
i'm thinking back,
thinking back
the past-
nothing has changed
(mind)
(love)
you have my heart
held fast

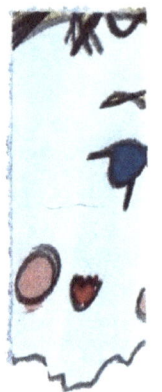

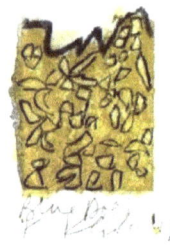

©1980 Karen Klosky

Dracmar, Queen of the Viper's Liar

will she appear
will she appear
yes!
she strikes again
in deadly fear

thrice upon my arm

she smote

each time i squeezed

close to her throat

escaped then

but now

vipress

in grandeur lies

succumbed

i die

to her song

and siren's cry

yes vipress extol

you have me

in your frozen fold

rejoicing now

inside my role

i pay the price

i am alone

your vanquished slave

soul spirit starved

a lonely guard

of dead

© 1979 Karen Klosky

I LOVE YOU

I WISH
WE HAD THE TIME
TO SAY
ALL THAT WE FEEL
TO LET EACH
EMOTION SURFACE
EXIST
AND THEN
BE REAL

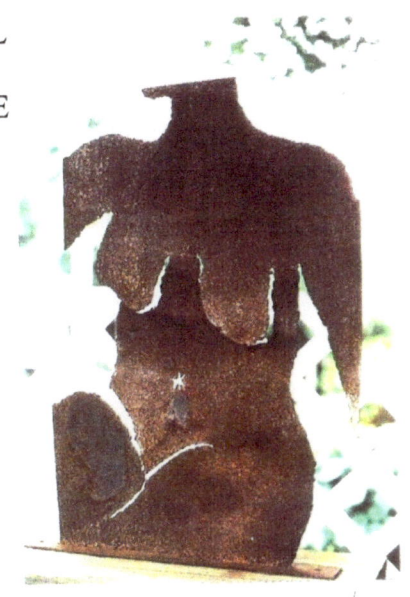

Time

Time is just
A repeat
Of time
And time again
All that
We once were
And will be
Again

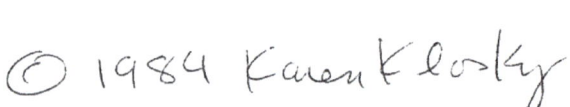

To D.C.B.

here's to my love

who's far away

across the dawn

and through the grey

marigolds and red maples

i saw today

(and through the grey

your presence pervades)

to you, love

who's beyond the call

of the light of day

i send you scarlet

russet rose

a color confetti

heyday

© 1980 Karen Klosky

all the words

all the words
in the world
big deal
all that really matters
is the sound

all the words
in the world
big deal
all that really matters
is the picture

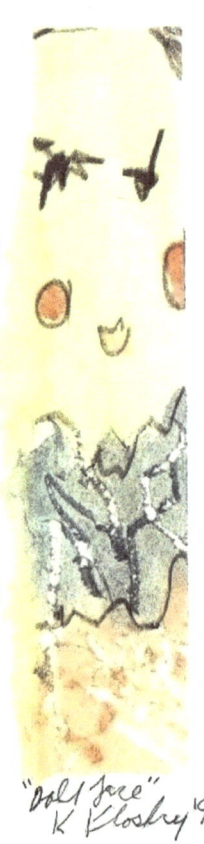

©1980 Karen Klosky

seventeen syllable poems

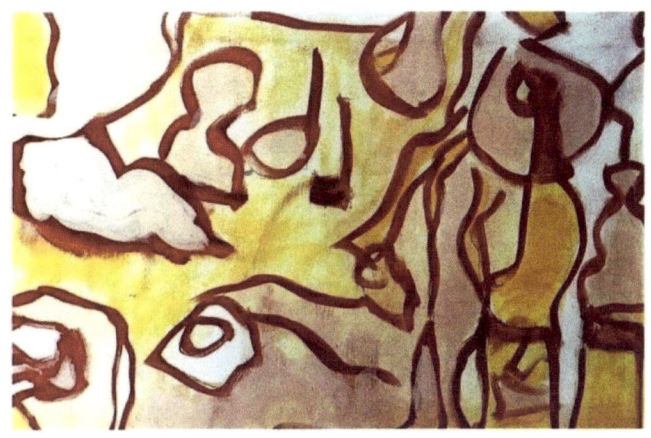

Blood of the Lamb

eye witness
stupidity walls
killing children fields
sorrow mothers

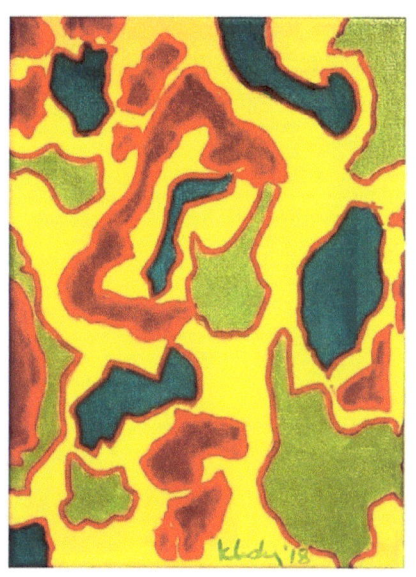

and all the blood
***

**and all the blood
of the children
flows
from columbine
to kosovo**

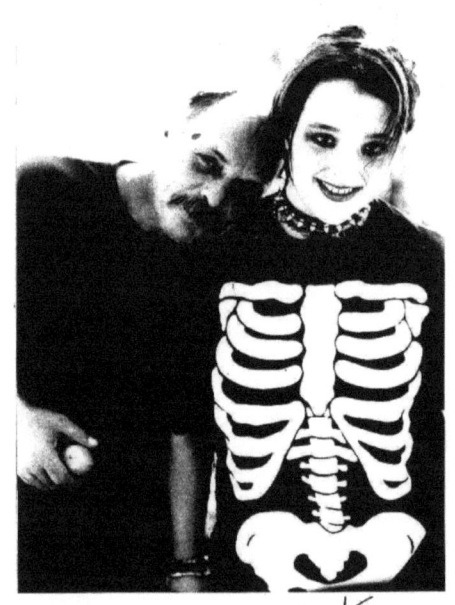

© 1999 Karen Klosky

to young mothers

put a halo
over your head
we know
who you are
our salvation

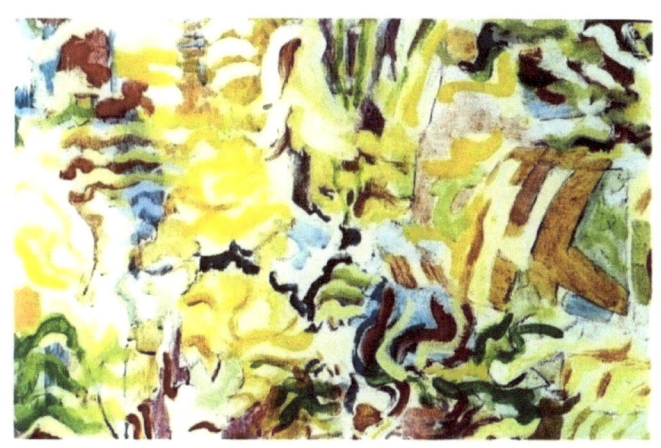

© 2000 Karen Klosky

sinister sister

i surprise myself
with the whip
belt
from the closet
where once he hid

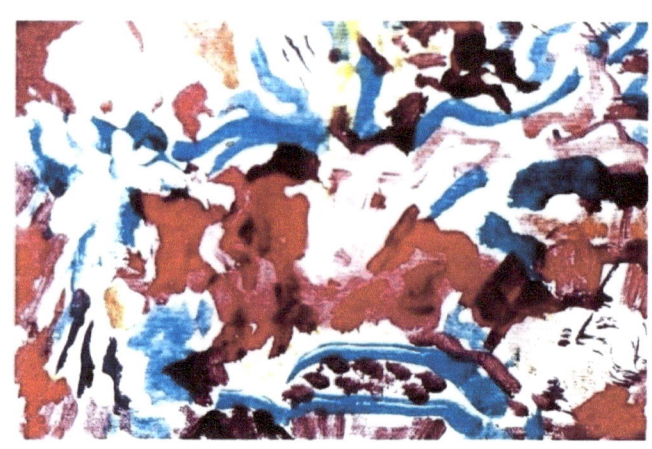

© 2000 Karen Klosky

lament
───────

snow white
and red rose
chose to go
on john-john's flight
now unfinished lives

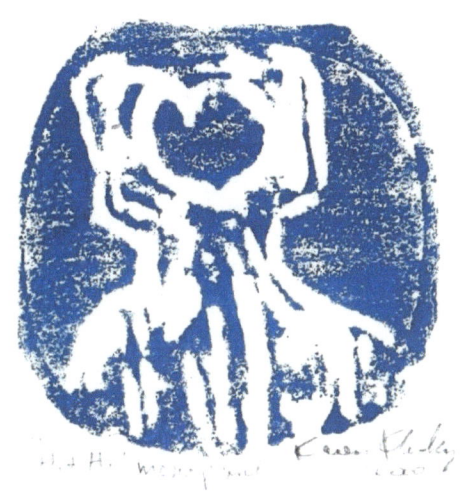

© 2000 Karen Klosky

dear senator
---

dear senator
what do i see
wounded child
HELP
go to next window

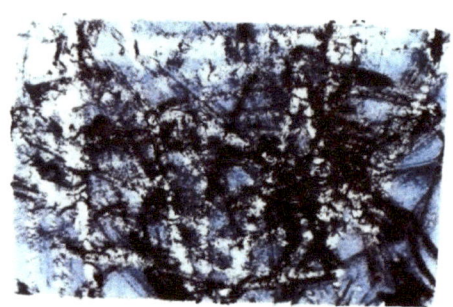

© 2000 Karen Klosky

daddy

**daddy
how could you
be so cruel
to a child
a being
so close to god**

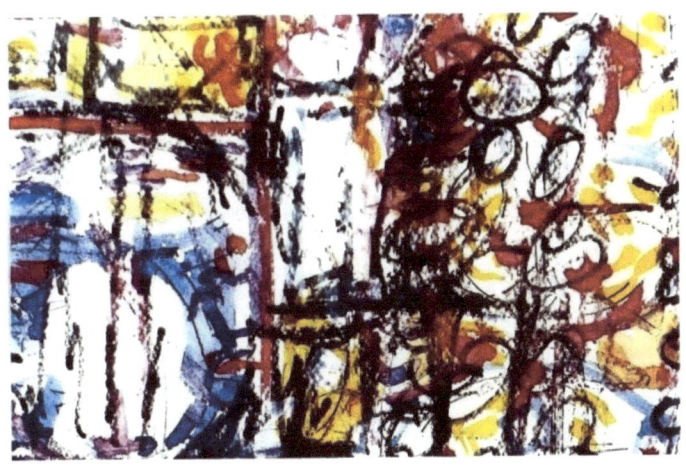

kiss

**i am forever
sustained
by our stolen
ardent kiss
on the bridge**

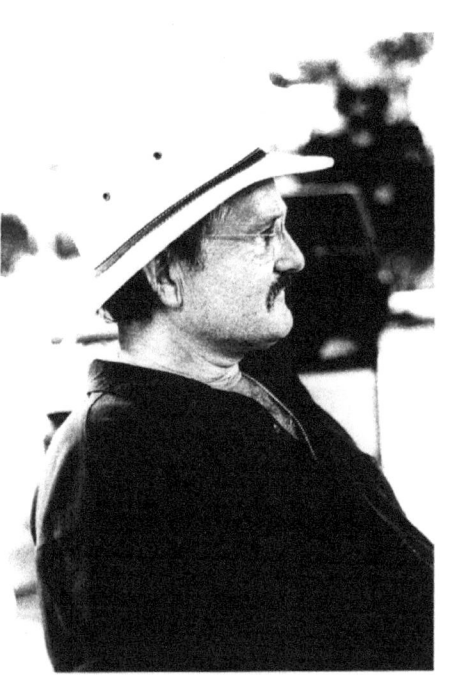

©2008 Karen Klosky

why say you

**why say you
win the war
all that's left
widows
orphans
disabled men**

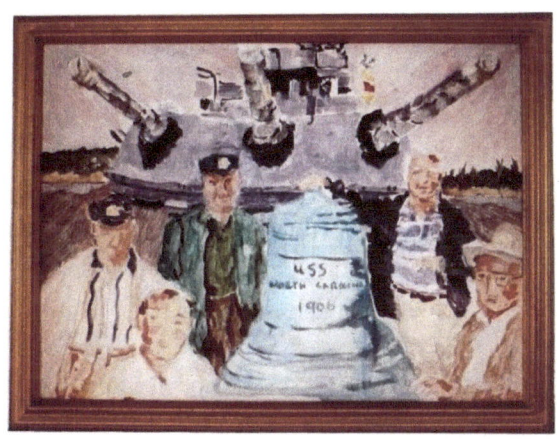

death

and i saw death
waiting beside me
getting ready
to close
the door

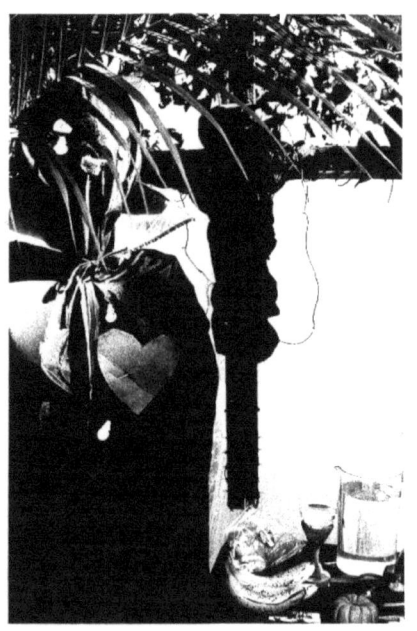

© 2007 Karen Klosky

Anger

**I
Make myself
Angry
It is thou
One must Answer
Not witholding**

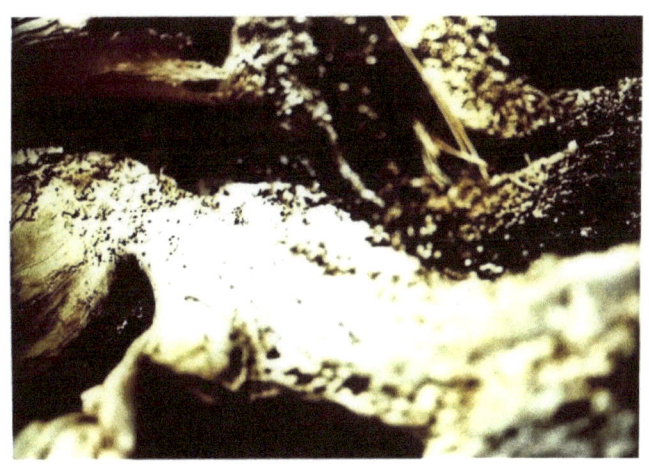

The Prayer

Full Moon
    Veined
And Veiled
    Through the Dark
Tree Limbs
    O Please
Bring World Peace

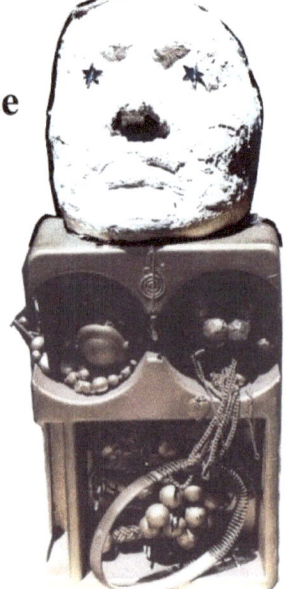

© 2008 K. Klosky

finale

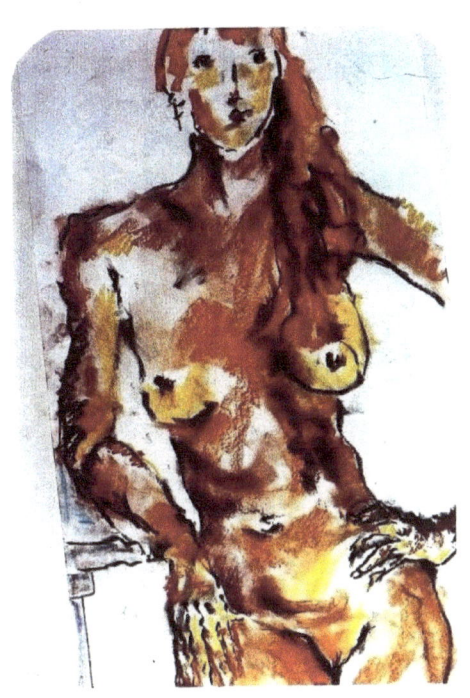

someone will be there

~

when i am gone

someone will feed the cats

someone will make the paintings

                that stand for what is right

someone will care about the animals

                trees lizards butterflys dolphins

someone will care about what happens

                to abused children mothers wives

someone will pray for the enlightenment of men

so i am not afraid

when i am gone

someone will love my son nieces brothers friends

someone will play music dance write the songs smile

someone will shine forth love
                         everyone sees feels shares
someone will admire
                         the beautiful blue sky clouds
someone will smell the roses honeysuckle
                         gardenias wine corks
so i am not afraid to go

when i am gone
someone will light the fire wear the pretty dress
someone will care about the
                         downtrodden forgotten lonely
someone will throw a party
                         sing happy birthday
someone will take care
someone will be there
so I am not afraid to go alone

TWO TUNES

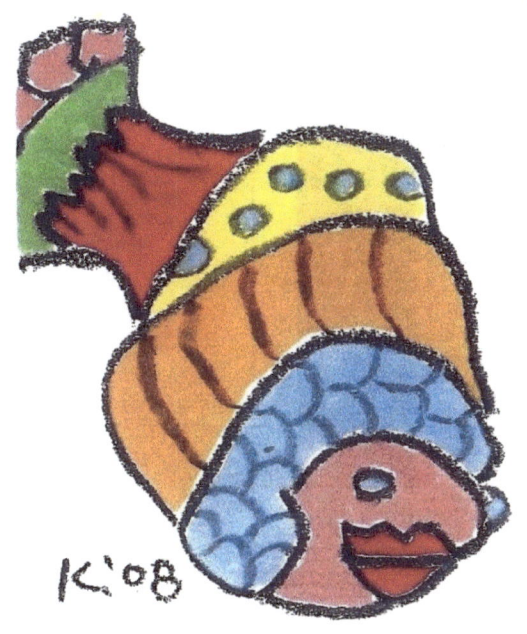

Tara's Tune

watch the spring turn to green
see the wind through the trees
birds call
i hear you sing

tara's tune
lazy afternoon
dandelions in profusion too
have you heard tara's tune

fresh mown hay
been hot all day
been thinkin' 'bout
cool water spout
in your eyes
reflections from the sky

tara's tune
hazy afternoon
dandelions
monarch butterfly
heaven is in your eyes

rainbow trout
grab your fishin' pole
sunlight streams
down through the cold
hours of time go drifting by

evening hues
sunset blues
crimson reds
soft breezes led
to the night the stars the moon and you
tara's tune
tara's tune
have you heard tara's tune

Written by Karen Klosky

Youtube: Tara's Tune
https://www.youtube.com/edit?video_id=HTIl9b0o0z0&video_referrer=watch

Dancin' in the Trees

By: Karen Klosky

Raccoons ticklin' my toes
Moonlight shines like snow
An amazing sight to see
Raccoons dancin' in the trees

Turkey Buzzards land one night
Loud raucous sound, quite a fright
Kinda spooky sight to see
Ninety buzzards dancin' in the trees

Got ten cats all 'round the house
All but one's quiet as a mouse
Such a happy sight to see
Ten cats dancin' in the trees

Neighbors dogs they like to bark
Chase the cats, invade the yard
Kinda crazy sight to see
Cats and dogs dancin' in the trees

Weeds growing all about
Do my best to pull them out
Makes no mind to me
Long as critters dancin' in the trees

Pileated 'Peckers doin' their love dance
Lifetime shot, just one chance
What a magic sight to see
Pileated 'Peckers dancin' in the trees

Little squirrels twitchin' their tails
Feed 'em every morning without fail
What a happy sight to see
All those squirrels dancin' in the trees

Pretty birds sing their song
Do my best to whistle along
Such a lovely sight to see
All those birds dancin' in the trees

Have a campfire now and then
Play guitar with all my friends
What a magic sight to see
All those hippies dancin' in the trees

Sometimes I have a smoke
Got a pipe take a toke
What a crazy sight to see
All those critters dancin' in the trees

Have a glass of red wine
Settles my heart, relaxes my mind
An upside place to be
All those critters dancin' in the trees

Find myself all alone
In a place I call my home
Peaceful and serene
Even with critters dancin' in the trees

Watch the sun going down
Golden light all around
A beautiful sight to see
Golden colors dancin' in the trees

Youtube: Dancin' in the Trees
https://www.youtube.com/edit?video_id=HTIl9b0o0z0&video_referrer=watch

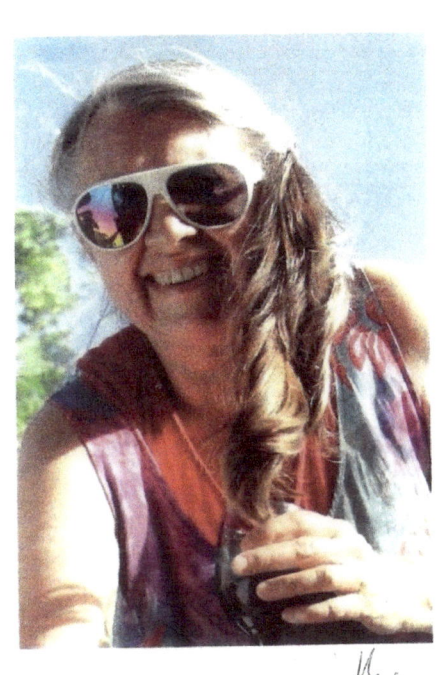

artist. poet. lyricist. author.

www.ingramcontent.com/pod-product-compliance
Lightning Source LLC
Chambersburg PA
CBHW040411220526
45473CB00004B/1202